Strange to Tell

A rich assortment of stories in verse to captivate all lovers of poetry who also delight in a tale well told.

Cover illustration by Desmond Clover

Strange to Tell

An anthology of narrative poems
compiled by
Dennis Saunders

Evans Brothers Limited, London

Published by Evans Brothers Limited
Montague House, Russell Square,
London, W.C.1.

Another for my daughter Clare
who enjoys a good story

Set in 11 on 13 pt Imprint and
printed in Great Britain by
Cox & Wyman Ltd,
London, Reading and Fakenham

CSD ISBN 0 237 44756 8   PRA 3589
PB   ISBN 0 237 44757 6

Contents

My Aunt

You've heard how a green thumb
Makes flowers come
Quite without toil
Out of any old soil.

Well, my Aunt's thumbs were green.
At a touch, she had blooms
Of prize Chrysanthemums –
The grandest ever seen.

People from miles around
Came to see those flowers
And were truly astounded
By her unusual powers.

One day a little weed
Pushed up to drink and feed
Among the pampered flowers
At her water-can showers.

Day by day it grew
With ragged leaves and bristles
Till it was tall as me or you –
It was a King of Thistles.

'Prizes for flowers are easy,'
My Aunt said in her pride.
'But was there ever such a weed
The whole world wide?'

She watered it, she tended it,
It grew alarmingly.
As if I had offended it,
It bristled over me.

'Oh Aunt!' I cried. 'Beware of that!
I saw it eat a bird.'
She went on polishing its points
As if she hadn't heard.

'Oh Aunt!' I cried. 'It has a flower
Like a lion's beard –'
Too late! It was devouring her
Just as I had feared!

Her feet were waving in the air –
But I shall not proceed.
Here ends the story of my Aunt
And her ungrateful weed.

Ted Hughes

Johnny Sands

A man whose name was Johnny Sands
   Had married Betty Hague,
And though she brought him gold and lands
   She proved a terrible plague.
For, O, she was a scolding wife,
   Full of caprice and whim;
He said that he was tired of life,
   And she was tired of him.

Says he, 'Then I will drown myself;
   The river runs below.'
Says she, 'Pray do, you silly elf,
   I wished it long ago.'
Says he, 'Upon the brink I'll stand,
   Do you run down the hill
And push me in with all your might.'
   Says she, 'My love, I will.'

'For fear that I should courage lack,
   And try to save my life,
Pray tie my hands behind my back.'
   'I will,' replied his wife.
She tied them fast as you may think,
   And when securely done,
'Now stand,' says she, 'upon the brink
   And I'll prepare to run.'

All down the hill his loving bride
   Now ran with all her force
To push him in – he stepped aside,
   And she fell in, of course.
Now splashing, dashing like a fish,
   'O, save me, Johnny Sands!'
'I can't, my dear, though much I wish,
   For you have tied my hands!'

Anon.

Colonel Fazackerley

Colonel Fazackerley Butterworth-Toast
Bought an old castle complete with a ghost,
But someone or other forgot to declare
To Colonel Fazack that the spectre was there.

On the very first evening, while waiting to dine,
The Colonel was taking a fine sherry wine,
When the ghost, with a furious flash and a flare,
Shot out of the chimney and shivered, 'Beware!'

Colonel Fazackerley put down his glass
And said, 'My dear fellow, that's really first class!
I just can't conceive how you do it at all.
I imagine you're going to a Fancy Dress Ball?'

At this, the dread ghost gave a withering cry.
Said the Colonel (his monocle firm in his eye),
'Now just how you do it I wish I could think.
Do sit down and tell me, and please have a drink.'

The ghost in his phosphorous cloak gave a roar
And floated about between ceiling and floor.
He walked through a wall and returned through a pane
And backed up the chimney and came down again.

Said the Colonel, 'With laughter I'm feeling quite weak!'
(As trickles of merriment ran down his cheek).
'My house-warming party I hope you won't spurn.
You *must* say you'll come and you'll give us a turn!'

At this, the poor spectre – quite out of his wits –
Proceeded to shake himself almost to bits.
He rattled his chains and he clattered his bones
And he filled the whole castle with mumbles and moans.

But Colonel Fazackerley, just as before,
Was simply delighted and called out, 'Encore!'
At which the ghost vanished, his efforts in vain,
And never was seen at the castle again.

'Oh dear, what a pity!' said Colonel Fazack.
'I don't know his name, so I can't call him back.'
And then with a smile that was hard to define,
Colonel Fazackerley went in to dine.

Charles Causley

The Stone Troll

Troll sat alone on his seat of stone,
And munched and mumbled a bare old bone;
   For many a year he had gnawed it near,
     For meat was hard to come by.
       Done by! Gum by!
   In a cave in the hills he dwelt alone,
     And meat was hard to come by.

Up came Tom with his big boots on.
Said he to Troll: 'Pray, what is yon?
   For it looks like the shin o' my nuncle Tim,
     As should be a-lyin' in graveyard.
       Caveyard! Paveyard!
   This many a year has Tim been gone,
     And I thought he were lyin' in graveyard'.

'My lad', said Troll, 'this bone I stole.
But what be bones that lie in a hole?
   Thy nuncle was dead as a lump o' lead,
     Afore I found his shinbone.
       Tinbone! Thinbone!
   He can spare a share for a poor old troll;
     For he don't need his shinbone'.

Said Tom: 'I don't see why the likes o' thee
Without axin' leave should go makin' free
    With the shank or the shin o' my father's kin;
        So hand the old bone over!
            Rover! Trover!
    Though dead he be, it belongs to he;
        So hand the old bone over!'

'For a couple o' pins', says Troll, and grins,
'I'll eat thee too, and gnaw thy shins.
    A bit o' fresh meat will go down sweet!
        I'll try my teeth on thee now.
            Hee now! See now!
    I'm tired o' gnawing old bones and skins;
        I've a mind to dine on thee now'.

But just as he thought his dinner was caught,
He found his hands had hold of naught.
    Before he could mind, Tom slipped behind
        And gave him the boot to larn him.
            Warn him! Darn him!
    A bump o' the boot on the seat, Tom thought,
        Would be the way to larn him.

But harder than stone is the flesh and bone
Of a troll that sits in the hills alone.
  As well set your boot to the mountain's root,
    For the seat of a troll don't feel it.
      Peel it! Heal it!
  Old Troll laughed, when he heard Tom groan,
    And he knew his toes could feel it.

Tom's leg is game, since home he came,
And his bootless foot is lasting lame;
  But Troll don't care, and he's still there
    With the bone he boned from its owner.
      Doner! Boner!
  Troll's old seat is still the same,
    And the bone he boned from its owner!

J. R. R. Tolkien

Framed in a First-Storey Winder

Framed in a first-storey winder of a burnin' buildin'
Appeared: A Yuman Ead!
'Jump into this net, wot we are 'oldin'
And yule be quite orl right!'

But 'e wouldn't jump ...

And the flames grew Igher and Igher and Igher.
(Phew!)

Framed in a second-storey winder of a burnin' buildin'
Appeared: A Yuman Ead!
'Jump into this net, wot we are 'oldin'
And yule be quite orl right!'

But 'e wouldn't jump ...

And the flames grew Igher and Igher and Igher
(Strewth!)

Framed in a third-storey winder of a burnin' buildin'
Appeared: A Yuman Ead!
'Jump into this net, wot we are 'oldin'
And yule be quite orl right!
Honest!'

And 'e jumped . . .

And 'e broke 'is bloomin' neck!

Anon.

Yarns

They have yarns
  Of a skyscraper so tall
    they had to put hinges
      on the two top stories
        so to let the moon go by,
Of one corn crop in Missouri when the roots
  went so deep and drew off so much water
    the Mississippi river bed that year was dry,
Of pancakes so thin
  they had only one side,
Of 'a fog so thick
  we shingled the barn
    and six feet out on the fog,'
Of Pecos Pete straddling a cyclone
  in Texas and riding it to the west coast
    where 'it rained out under him,'
Of the man who drove a swarm of bees
  across the Rocky Mountains and the Desert
    'and didn't lose a bee.'
Of a mountain railroad curve
  where the engineer in his cab can touch the caboose
    and spit in the conductor's eye,
Of the boy who climbed a cornstalk
  growing so fast he would have starved to death
    if they hadn't shot biscuits up to him,

Of the old man's whiskers:
  'When the wind was with him
    his whiskers arrived a day before he did,'
Of the hen laying a square egg
  and cackling, 'Ouch!' and of hens laying eggs
    with the dates printed on them,
Of the ship captain's shadow:
  it froze to the deck
    one cold winter night,
Of mutineers on that same ship
  put to chipping rust
    with rubber hammers,
Of the sheep-counter
  who was fast and accurate:
    'I just count their feet and divide by four,'
Of the man so tall
  he must climb a ladder
    to shave himself,
Of the runt so teeny-weeny
  it takes two men and a boy
    to see him,
Of mosquitoes:
  one can kill a dog,
    two of them a man,

Of a cyclone that sucked cookstoves
   out of the kitchen, up the chimney flue,
      and on to the next town,
Of the same cyclone picking up wagon-tracks
   in Nebraska and dropping them
      over the Dakotas,
Of the hook-and-eye snake
   unlocking itself into forty pieces, each piece two inches long,
      then in nine seconds flat snapping itself together again,
Of the watch swallowed by the cow:
   when they butchered her a year later the watch was running
      and had the correct time,
Of horned snakes, hoop snakes that roll themselves
   where they want to go, and rattlesnakes
      carrying bells instead of rattles on their tails,
Of the herd of cattle in California
   getting lost in a giant redwood tree
      that had been hollowed out,
Of the man who killed a snake
   by putting its tail in its mouth
      so it swallowed itself,
Of railroad trains whizzing along
   so fast they reached the station
      before the whistle,

Of pigs so thin
   the farmer had to tie knots
      in their tails
         to keep them from crawling
            through the cracks in their pens,
Of Paul Bunyan's big blue ox, Babe,
   measuring between the eyes
      forty-two axe-handles and a plug
         of Star tobacco exactly,
Of John Henry's hammer
   and the curve of its swing
      and his singing of it
         as 'a rainbow round my shoulder.' They have yarns ...

Carl Sandburg

The Alarmed Skipper

Many a long, long year ago,
Nantucket skippers had a plan
Of finding out, though 'lying low,'
How near New York their schooners ran.

They greased the lead before it fell,
And then, by sounding through the night,
Knowing the soil that stuck, so well,
They always guessed their reckoning right.

A skipper gray, whose eyes were dim,
Could tell, by *tasting*, just the spot,
And so below he'd 'dowse the glim' –
After, of course, his 'something hot.'

Snug in his berth, at eight o'clock,
This ancient skipper might be found;
No matter how his craft would rock,
He slept – for skippers' naps are sound!

The watch on deck would now and then
Run down and wake him, with the lead;
He'd up, and taste, and tell the men
How many miles they went ahead.

One night, 'twas Jonathan Marden's watch,
A curious wag – the peddler's son –
And so he mused (the wanton wretch),
'To-night I'll have a grain of fun.

'We're all a set of stupid fools
To think the skipper knows by *tasting*
What ground he's on – Nantucket schools
Don't teach such stuff, with all their basting!'

And so he took the well-greased lead
And rubbed it o'er a box of earth
That stood on deck – a parsnip-bed –
And then he sought the skipper's berth.

'Where are we now, sir? Please to taste.'
The skipper yawned, put out his tongue,
Then ope'd his eyes in wondrous haste,
And then upon the floor he sprung!

The skipper stormed and tore his hair,
Thrust on his boots, and roared to Marden,
'Nantucket's sunk; and here we are
Right over old Marm Hackett's garden!'

James Thomas Fields

Get Up and Bar the Door

It fell about the Martinmas time,
    And a gay time it was then,
When our good wife got puddings to make,
    And she's boiled them in the pan.

The wind so cold blew south and north,
    And blew into the floor;
Quoth our goodman to our goodwife,
    'Get up and bar the door.'

'My hand is in my household work,
    Goodman, as ye may see;
And it will not be barred for a hundred years,
    If it's to be barred by me!'

They made a pact between them both,
    They made it firm and sure,
That whosoe'er should speak the first,
    Should rise and bar the door.

Then by there came two gentlemen,
    At twelve o'clock at night,
And they could see neither house nor hall,
    Nor coal nor candlelight.

'Now whether is this a rich man's house,
    Or whether is it a poor?'
But never a word would one of them speak,
    For barring of the door.

The guests they ate the white puddings,
    And then they ate the black;
Tho' much the goodwife thought to herself,
    Yet never a word she spake.

Then said one stranger to the other,
    'Here, man, take ye my knife;
Do ye take off the old man's beard,
    And I'll kiss the goodwife.'

'There's no hot water to scrape it off,
    And what shall we do then?'
'Then why not use the pudding broth,
    That boils into the pan?'

O up then started our goodman,
    An angry man was he;
'Will ye kiss my wife before my eyes!
    And with pudding broth scald me!'

Then up and started our goodwife,
    Gave three skips on the floor:
'Goodman, you've spoken the very first word!
    Get up and bar the door!'

                                    Anon.

Welsh Incident

'That was nothing to what things came out
From the sea-caves of Criccieth yonder.'
'What were they? Mermaids? dragons? ghosts?'
'Nothing at all of any things like that.'
'What were they, then?'

                  'All sorts of queer things,
Things never seen or heard or written about,
Very strange, un-Welsh, utterly peculiar
Things. Oh, solid enough they seemed to touch,
Had anyone dared it. Marvellous creation,
All various shapes and sizes and no sizes,
All new, each perfectly unlike his neighbour,
Though all came moving slowly out together.'
'Describe just one of them.'

                    'I am unable.'
'What were their colours?'

                    'Mostly nameless colours,
Colours you'd like to see; but one was puce
Or perhaps more like crimson, but not purplish.
Some had no colour.'

                'Tell me, had they legs?'
'Not a leg or foot among them that I saw.'
'But did these things come out in any order?
What o'clock was it? What was the day of the week?
Who else was present? How was the weather?'
'I was coming to that. It was half-past three
On Easter Tuesday last. The sun was shining.

The Harlech Silver Band played *Marchog Jesu*
On thirty-seven shimmering instruments,
Collecting for Caernarvon's (Fever) Hospital Fund.
The population of Pwllheli, Criccieth,
Portmadoc, Borth, Tremadoc, Penrhyndeudraeth,
Were all assembled. Criccieth's mayor addressed them
First in good Welsh and then in fluent English,
Twisting his fingers in his chain of office,
Welcoming the things. They came out on the sand,
Not keeping time to the band, moving seaward
Silently at a snail's pace. But at last
The most odd, indescribable thing of all
Which hardly one man there could see for wonder
Did something recognisably a something.'
'Well, what?'
                    'It made a noise.'
                              'A frightening noise?'
'No, no.'
          'A musical noise? A noise of scuffling?'
'No, but a very loud, respectable noise –
Like groaning to oneself on Sunday morning
In Chapel, close before the second psalm.'
'What did the mayor do?'
                              'I was coming to that.'

                                        Robert Graves

The David Jazz

David was a Young Blood, David was a striplin',
Looked like the Jungle Boy, yarned about by Kiplin' –
Looked like a Jungle Boy, sang like a bird,
Fought like a tiger when his temper got stirred.

David was a-tendin' the sheep for his Pa,
Somebody hollered to him – that was his Ma –
'Run down to camp with this little bitta snack,
Give it to your brothers, an' hurry right back.'

David took the luncheon, and off he hurried,
There he saw the Isra'lites lookin' right worried.
Asked 'em what's the matter – they pointed to the prairie –
There he saw a sight to make a elephant scary!
There he saw Goliath,
Champion o' Gath,
Howlin' in his anger,
Roarin' in his wrath;
Stronger than a lion,
Taller than a tree –
David had to tiptoe to reach to his knee!

'Come on,' says the giant, a-ragin' and a-stridin' –
'Drag out your champions from the holes where they're hidin',
Drag out your strong men from underneath their bunks,
And I'll give 'em to the buzzards, an' the lizards, an' the skunks.'

David heard him braggin', and he said, 'I declare,
The great big lummox got 'em buffaloed for fair.'
Goes to the brook, and he picks him out a pebble,
Smooth as a goose-egg an' hard as the debbil.
Starts for the giant, dancin' on his toes,
Whirlin' his sling-shot and singin' as he goes –
'Better get organised, for here I come a-hoppin',
Time's gettin' short, and hell am a-poppin'.
Hell am a-poppin' and trouble am a-brewin',
Nothin's going to save you from Big Red Ruin.
Trouble am a-brewin' and Death am distillin' –
Look out, you Philistine – there's gwine ter be a killin'!'

Giant looks at David an' he lets out a laugh –
Acts like a tiger bein' sassed by a calf;
Laughs like a hyena, grins from ear to ear,
Rattles on his armour with his ten-foot spear,
Starts out for David, bangin' and a-clankin' –
'Come on, l'il infant, you're a-goin' to get a spankin'!'
David takes his sling-shot, swings it round his head,
Lets fly a pebble – and the gi'nt drops dead!

Moral

Big men, little men, houses and cars,
Widders and winders and porcelain jars –
Nothin' ain't safe from damage an' shocks,
When the neighbourhood chillen gets to slingin' rocks!

Edwin Meade Robinson

Nursery Rhyme of Innocence and Experience

I had a silver penny
   And an apricot tree
And I said to the sailor
   On the white quay

'Sailor O sailor
   Will you bring me
If I give you my penny
   And my apricot tree

A fez from Algeria
   An Arab drum to beat
A little gilt sword
   And a parakeet?'

And he smiled and he kissed me
   As strong as death
And I saw his red tongue
   And I felt his sweet breath

'You may keep your penny
   And your apricot tree
And I'll bring your presents
   Back from the sea.'

O the ship dipped down
  On the rim of the sky
And I waited while three
  Long summers went by

Then one steel morning
  On the white quay
I saw a grey ship
  Come in from sea

Slowly she came
  Across the bay
For her flashing rigging
  Was shot away

All round her wake
  The seabirds cried
And flew in and out
  Of the hole in her side

Slowly she came
  In the path of the sun
And I heard the sound
  Of a distant gun

And a stranger came running
    Up to me
From the deck of the ship
    And he said, said he

'*O are you the boy*
    Who would wait on the quay
With the silver penny
    And the apricot tree?

I've a plum-coloured fez
    And a drum for thee
And a sword and a parakeet
    From over the sea.'

'O where is the sailor
    With bold red hair?
And what is that volley
    On the bright air?

'O where are the other
    Girls and boys?
And why have you brought me
    Children's toys?'

Charles Causley

Legend

The blacksmith's boy went out with a rifle
and a black dog running behind.
Cobwebs snatched at his feet,
rivers hindered him,
thorn branches caught at his eyes to make him blind
and the sky turned into an unlucky opal,
but he didn't mind,
I can break branches, I can swim rivers, I can stare out any spider I
    meet,
said he to his dog and his rifle.

The blacksmith's boy went over the paddocks
with his old black hat on his head.
Mountains jumped in his way,
rocks rolled down on him,
and the old crow cried, You'll soon be dead.
And the rain came down like mattocks.
But he only said
I can climb mountains, I can dodge rocks, I can shoot an old crow
    any day,
And he went on over the paddocks.

mattocks: pick-axes or hammers

When he came to the end of the day the sun began falling.
Up came the night ready to swallow him,
like the barrel of a gun,
like an old black hat,
like a black dog hungry to follow him.
Then the pigeon, the magpie and the dove began wailing
and the grass lay down to pillow him.
His rifle broke, his hat blew away and his dog was gone,
and the sun was falling.

But in front of the night the rainbow stood on the mountain
just as his heart foretold.
He ran like a hare,
he climbed like a fox;
he caught it in his hands, the colours and the cold –
like a bar of ice, like the column of a fountain,
like a ring of gold.
The pigeon, the magpie and the dove flew up to stare,
and the grass stood up again on the mountain.

The blacksmith's boy hung the rainbow on his shoulder
instead of his broken gun.
Lizards ran out to see,
snakes made way for him,
and the rainbow shone as brightly as the sun.
All the world said, Nobody is braver, nobody is bolder,
nobody else has done
anything to equal it.
He went home as bold as he could be
with the swinging rainbow on his shoulder.

Judith Wright

The History of the Flood

Bang Bang Bang
Said the nails in the Ark.

It's getting rather dark
Said the nails in the Ark.

For the rain is coming down
Said the nails in the Ark.

And you're all going to drown
Said the nails in the Ark.

Dark and black as sin
Said the nails in the Ark.

So won't you all come in
Said the nails in the Ark.

But only two by two
Said the nails in the Ark.

So they came in two by two,
The elephant, the kangaroo,
And the gnu,
And the little tiny shrew.

Then the birds
Flocked in like wingèd words:
Two racket-tailed motmots, two macaws,
Two nuthatches and two
Little bright robins.

And the reptiles: the gila monster, the slow-worm,
The green mamba, the cottonmouth, and the alligator –
All squirmed in;
And after a very lengthy walk,
Two giant Galapagos tortoises.

And the insects in their hierarchies:
A queen ant, a king ant, a queen wasp, a king wasp,
A queen bee, a king bee,
And all the beetles, bugs, and mosquitoes,
Cascaded in like glittering, murmurous jewels.

But the fish had their wish;
For the rain came down.
People began to drown:
The wicked, the rich –
They gasped out bubbles of pure gold,
Which exhalations
Rose to the constellations.

So for forty days and forty nights
They were on the waste of waters
In those cramped quarters.
It was very dark, damp and lonely.
There was nothing to see, but only
The rain which continued to drop.
It did not stop.

So Noah sent forth a raven. The raven said 'Kark!
I will not go back to the Ark.'
The raven was footloose,
He fed on the bodies of the rich –
Rich with vitamins and goo.
They had become bloated,
And everywhere they floated.
The raven's heart was black,
He did not come back.
It was not a nice thing to do:

Which is why the raven is a token of wrath,
And creaks like a rusty gate
When he crosses your path; and Fate
Will grant you no luck that day:
The raven is fey:
You were meant to have a scare.
Fortunately in England
The raven is rather rare.

Then Noah sent forth a dove
She did not want to rove.
She longed for her love –
The other turtle dove –
(For her no other dove!)
She brought back a twig from an olive-tree.
There is no more beautiful tree
Anywhere on the earth,
Even when it comes to birth
From six weeks under the sea.

She did not want to rove.
She wanted to take her rest,
And to build herself a nest
All in the olive grove.
She wanted to make love.
She thought that was the best.

The dove was not a rover;
So they knew that the rain was over.
Noah and his wife got out
(They had become rather stout)
And Japhet, Ham, and Shem.
(The same could be said of them.)
They looked up at the sky.
The earth was becoming dry.

Then the animals came ashore –
There were more of them than before:
There were two dogs and a litter of puppies;
There were a tom-cat and two tib-cats
And two litters of kittens – cats
Do not obey regulations;
And, as you might expect,
A quantity of rabbits.

God put a rainbow in the sky.
They wondered what it was for.
There had never been a rainbow before.
The rainbow was a sign;
It looked like a neon sign –
Seven colours arched in the skies:
What should it publicize?
They looked up with wondering eyes.

It advertises Mercy
Said the nails in the Ark.

Mercy Mercy Mercy
Said the nails in the Ark.

Our God is merciful
Said the nails in the Ark.

Merciful and gracious
Bang Bang Bang Bang.

John Heath-Stubbs

The Rider at the Gate

A windy night was blowing on Rome,
The cressets guttered on Caesar's home,
The fish-boats, moored at the bridge, were breaking
The rush of the river to yellow foam.

The hinges whined to the shutters shaking,
When clip-clop-clep came a horse-hoof raking
The stones of the road at Caesar's gate;
The spear-butts jarred at the guard's awaking.

'Who goes there?' said the guard at the gate.
'What is the news, that you ride so late?'
'News most pressing, that must be spoken
To Caesar alone and that cannot wait.'

'The Caesar sleeps; you must show a token
That the news suffice that he be awoken.
What is the news, and whence do you come?
For no light cause may his sleep be broken.'

'Out of the dark of the sands I come,
From the dark of death with news for Rome.
A word so fell that it must be uttered
Though it strike the soul of the Caesar dumb.'

Caesar turned in his bed and muttered,
With a struggle for breath the lamp-flame guttered;
Calpurnia heard her husband moan: 'The house is falling,
The beaten men come into their own.'

'Speak your word,' said the guard at the gate;
'Yes, but bear it to Caesar straight,
Say, "Your murderer's knives are honing,
Your killer's gang is lying in wait."

'Out of the wind that is blowing and moaning,
Through the city palace and the country loaning,
I cry, "For the world's sake, Caesar, beware,
And take this warning as my atoning.

'"Beware of the Court, of the palace stair,
Of the downcast friend who speaks so fair,
Keep from the Senate, for Death is going
On many men's feet to meet you there."

'I, who am dead, have ways of knowing
Of the crop of death that the quick are sowing.
I, who was Pompey, cry it aloud
From the dark of death, from the wind blowing.

'I, who was Pompey, once was proud,
Now I lie in the sand without a shroud;
I cry to Caesar out of my pain,
"Caesar, beware, your death is vowed."'

The light grew grey on the window-pane,
The windcocks swung in a burst of rain,
The window of Caesar flung unshuttered,
The horse-hoofs died into wind again.

Caesar turned in his bed and muttered,
With a struggle for breath the lamp-flame guttered;
Calpurnia heard her husband moan: 'The house is falling,
The beaten men come into their own.'

John Masefield

Flannan Isle

'Though three men dwell on Flannan Isle
To keep the lamp alight,
As we steered under the lee, we caught
No glimmer through the night.'

A passing ship at dawn had brought
The news, and quickly we set sail,
To find out what strange thing might ail
The keepers of the deep-sea light.

The winter day broke blue and bright
With glancing sun and glancing spray
While o'er the swell our boat made way,
As gallant as a gull in flight.

But as we neared the lonely Isle
And looked up at the naked height,
And saw the lighthouse towering white
With blinded lantern, that all night
Had never shot a spark
Of comfort through the dark,
So ghostly in the cold sunlight
It seemed that we were struck the while
With wonder all too dread for words.

And, as into the tiny creek
We stole beneath the hanging crag,
We saw three queer black ugly birds –
Too big by far in my belief,
For cormorant or shag –
Like seamen sitting bolt-upright
Up on a half-tide reef:
But, as we neared, they plunged from sight
Without a sound or spurt of white.

And still too mazed to speak,
We landed; and made fast the boat;
And climbed the track in single file,
Each wishing he was safe afloat
On any sea, however far,
So it be far from Flannan Isle:

And still we seemed to climb and climb
As though we'd lost all count of time
And so must climb for evermore.
Yet, all too soon, we reached the door –
The black, sun-blistered lighthouse-door,
That gaped for us ajar.

As, on the threshold, for a spell
We paused, we seemed to breathe the smell
Of limewash and of tar,
Familiar as our daily breath,
As though 'twere some strange scent of death;
And so yet wondering, side by side
We stood a moment still tongue-tied;
And each with black foreboding eyed
The door, ere we should fling it wide
To leave the sunlight for the gloom:
Till, plucking courage up, at last
Hard on each other's heels we passed
Into the living-room.

Yet, as we crowded through the door
We only saw a table, spread
For dinner, meat and cheese and bread;
But all untouched; and no one there:
As though, when they sat down to eat,
Ere they could even taste,
Alarm had come; and they in haste
Had risen and left the bread and meat,
For at the table-head a chair
Lay tumbled on the floor.

We listened, but we only heard
The feeble chirping of a bird
That starved upon its perch;
And, listening still, without a word
We set about our hopeless search.
We hunted high, we hunted low,
And soon ransacked the empty house;
Then o'er the Island, to and fro
We ranged, to listen and to look
In every cranny, cleft or nook
That might have hid a bird or mouse:

But though we searched from shore to shore
We found no sign in any place,
And soon again stood face to face
Before the gaping door,
And stole into the room once more
As frightened children steal.

Ay, though we hunted high and low
And hunted everywhere,
Of the three men's fate we found no trace
Of any kind in any place
But a door ajar, and an untouched meal,
And an overtoppled chair.

And as we listened in the gloom
Of that forsaken living-room –
A chill clutch on our breath –
We thought how ill-chance came to all
Who kept the Flannan Light,
And how the rock had been the death
Of many a likely lad –
How six had come to a sudden end
And three had gone stark mad,
And one whom we'd all known as friend,
Had leapt from the lantern one still night,
And fallen dead by the lighthouse wall –
And long we thought
On the three we sought,
And on what might yet befall.

Like curs a glance has brought to heel
We listened, flinching there,
And looked, and looked, on the untouched meal,
And the overtoppled chair.

We seemed to stand for an endless while,
Though still no word was said,
Three men alive on Flannan Isle
Who thought on three men dead.

Wilfred Wilson Gibson

Ballad of Springhill

In the town of Springhill, Nova Scotia,
　　Down in the dark of the Cumberland mine,
There's blood on the coal and the miners lie
　　In the roads that never saw sun nor sky,
　　The roads that never saw sun nor sky.

In the town of Springhill you don't sleep easy
　　Often the earth will tremble and roll.
When the earth is restless, miners die,
　　Bone and blood is the price of coal.

In the town of Springhill, Nova Scotia,
　　Late in the year of fifty-eight,
Day still comes and the sun still shines,
　　But it's dark as the grave in the Cumberland mine.

Down at the coal-face, miners working,
　　Rattle of the belt and the cutter's blade,
Rumble of rock and the walls close round,
　　The living and the dead men two miles down.

Twelve men lay two miles from the pitshaft,
　　Twelve men lay in the dark and sang.
Long hot days in the miner's tomb,
　　It was three feet high and a hundred long.

Three days passed and the lamps gave out.
  And Caleb Rushton he up and said:
There's no more water nor light nor bread,
  So we'll live on songs and hope instead.

Listen for the shouts of the barefaced miners,
  Listen through the rubble for a rescue team,
Six-hundred feet of coal and slag,
  Hope imprisoned in a three-foot seam.

Eight days passed and some were rescued
  Leaving the dead to lie alone,
Through all their lives they dug a grave
  Two miles of earth for a marking stone.

Ewan MacColl and Peggy Seeger

Ghost Village by the Shore

There's a village and a harbour where the tide groans night and day,
A place where trippers never come and where no children play
With the shifting, muddy sands that are silting up the bay.

And the village is half-empty and those who live there yet
Sit huddled by their fires as if trying to forget
All the sorrow of a lifetime and the ghosts for whom they fret.

For the harbour did not always lie abandoned, and the tide
Bore proudly once these boats that now lie rotting on their side,
And the laughing men who sailed in them were worth a nation's
pride.

But when the grim night fell that struck them old at one swift blow,
Of all who nurse their sorrow in the crumbling village now
Not one had a streak of grey in her hair, or wrinkle on her brow.

All day before, the slate-grey sea heaved up at the slate-grey sky,
And the shore-bound fishermen mending their tackle watched with a
wary eye
Where the tilting ocean fumed and foamed like a beast in agony.

And at twilight when the western clouds were stained as if with blood
The fishermen met in the Harbour Inn, and their leader spoke where
   he stood:
'We'll keep a watch tonight by turns, so sleep while the going's good.'

The wind howled round the shuttered inn, and tore down the sign
   where it hung,
And a short while they stayed to drink a tot, and a merry song was
   sung;
Then they suddenly went quiet as the tocsin bell was rung.

And white-faced in the dark they loosed their boats and let them slip
Into the sea's black torrent while, exploding like a whip,
The storm alive with lightning lashed and broke the sinking ship.

And lightning, too, revealed to those who knelt upon the shore
The sullen anger of the waves while for a time they bore
Young sweethearts, husbands, brothers, all straining at the oar.

And like a god, the ocean first took in his mighty hand
A score of men who in pure love defied his great command –
And in contempt he smashed them and the little boats they manned.

From the ship that went down not a man, not a rat got away,
And of those who went out in the dark, never one saw the day,
Though later the tide swept their bodies back into the bay.

There's a village and a harbour where the midnight tide still groans
For the brave men it has drowned, and with eyes as still as stones
The villagers lie waiting for the wind that stirs and moans.

For the wind, the wind comes drowning a merry song that's sung,
And it tears the creaking inn-sign from the place where it is hung,
And blows dead faces through the dark while the tocsin bell is rung.

Raymond Wilson

The Griesly Wife

'Lie still, my newly married wife,
  Lie easy as you can.
You're young and ill accustomed yet
  To sleeping with a man.'

The snow lay thick, the moon was full
  And shone across the floor.
The young wife went with never a word
  Barefooted to the door.

He up and followed sure and fast,
  The moon shone clear and white.
But before his coat was on his back
  His wife was out of sight.

He trod the trail wherever it turned
  By many a mound and scree,
And still the barefoot track led on
  And an angry man was he.

He followed fast, he followed slow,
  And still he called her name,
But only the dingoes of the hills
  Yowled back at him again.

His hair stood up along his neck,
　His angry mind was gone,
For the track of the two bare feet gave out
　And a four-foot track went on.

Her nightgown lay upon the snow
　As it might upon the sheet,
But the track that led on from where it lay
　Was never of human feet.

His heart turned over in his chest,
　He looked from side to side,
And he thought more of his gumwood fire
　Than he did of his griesly bride.

And first he started walking back
　And then began to run
And his quarry wheeled at the end of her track
　And hunted him in turn.

Oh, long the fire may burn for him
　And open stand the door,
And long the bed may wait empty:
　He'll not be back any more.

　　　　　　　　　　John Manifold

The White-footed Deer

It was a hundred years ago,
  When, by the woodland ways,
The traveller saw the wild deer drink,
  Or crop the birchen sprays.

Beneath a hill, whose rocky side
  O'erbrowed a grassy mead,
And fenced a cottage from the wind,
  A deer was wont to feed.

She only came when on the cliffs
  The evening moonlight lay,
And no man knew the secret haunts
  In which she walked by day.

White were her feet, her forehead showed
  A spot of silvery white,
That seemed to glimmer like a star
  In autumn's hazy night.

And here, when sang the whippoorwill,
  She cropped the sprouting leaves,
And here her rustling steps were heard
  On still October eves.

But when the broad midsummer moon
   Rose o'er that grassy lawn,
Beside the silver-footed deer
   There grazed a spotted fawn.

The cottage dame forbade her son
   To aim the rifle here;
'It were a sin,' she said, 'to harm
   Or fright that friendly deer.

'This spot has been my pleasant home
   Ten peaceful years and more;
And ever when the moonlight shines,
   She feeds before our door.

'The red men say that here she walked
   A thousand moons ago;
They never raise the war-whoop here,
   And never twang the bow.

'I love to watch her as she feeds,
   And think that all is well,
While such a gentle creature haunts
   The place in which we dwell.'

The youth obeyed, and sought for game
    In forest far away,
Where deep in silence and in moss,
    The ancient woodland lay.

But once, in autumn's golden time,
    He ranged the wild in vain,
Nor roused the pheasant nor the deer,
    And wandered home again.

The crescent moon and crimson eve
    Shone with a mingling light;
The deer upon the grassy mead
    Was feeding full in sight.

He raised the rifle to his eye,
    And from the cliffs around
A sudden echo, shrill and sharp,
    Gave back its deadly sound.

Away into the neighbouring wood
    The startled creature flew,
And crimson drops at morning lay
    Amid the glimmering dew.

Next evening shone the waxing moon
    As sweetly as before;
The deer upon the grassy mead
    Was seen again no more.

But ere that crescent moon was old
    By night the red men came,
And burnt the cottage to the ground,
    And slew the youth and dame.

Now woods have overgrown the mead,
    And hid the cliffs from sight;
There shrieks the hovering hawk at noon,
    And prowls the fox at night.

William Cullen Bryant

Take Heart, Sweet Mary

Joseph :   Take heart, the journey's ended,
         I see the twinkling lights
Where we shall be befriended
         On this the night of nights.

Mary :   Now praise the Lord that led us
         So safe unto the town,
Where men will feed and bed us,
         And I can lay me down.

Joseph :   And how then shall we praise Him?
         Alas, my heart is sore
That we no gifts can raise Him
         Who are so very poor.

Mary :   We have as much as any
         That on the earth do live,
Although we have no penny
         We have ourselves to give.

Joseph :   Look yonder, wife, look yonder!
         An hostelry I see
Where travellers that wander
         Will very welcome be.

Mary : The house is tall and stately,
    The door stands open thus,
Yet, husband, I fear greatly
    That Inn is not for us.

Joseph : God save you, gentle master!
    Your littlest room indeed
With plainest walls of plaster
    To-night will serve our need.

Host : For lordings and for ladies
    I've lodging and to spare,
For you and yonder maid is
    No closet anywhere.

Joseph : Take heart, take heart, sweet Mary,
    Another Inn I spy
Whose Host will not be chary
    To let us easy lie.

Mary : Oh aid me, I am ailing,
    My strength is nearly gone,
I feel my limbs are failing,
    And yet we must go on.

Joseph :   God save you, Hostess, kindly!
                I pray you, house my wife
            Who bears beside me blindly
                The burden of her life.

Hostess :   My guests are rich men's daughters
                And sons, I'd have you know!
            Seek out the poorer quarters
                Where ragged people go.

Joseph :   Good sir, my wife's in labour,
                Some corner let us keep.

Host :   Not I! Knock up my neighbour,
                And as for me, I'll sleep.

Mary :   In all the lighted city
                Where rich men welcome win,
            Will not one house for pity
                Take two poor strangers in?

Joseph :   Good woman, I implore you
                Afford my wife a bed.

Hostess :   Nay, nay, I've nothing for you
                Except the cattle-shed.

Mary : Then gladly in the manger
     Our bodies we will house,
Since men to-night are stranger
     Than asses are and cows.

Joseph : Take heart, take heart, sweet Mary,
     The cattle are our friends.
Lie down, lie down, sweet Mary,
     For here the journey ends.

Mary : Now praise the Lord that found me
     This shelter in the town,
Where I with friends around me
     May lay my burden down.

Eleanor Farjeon
(Freely adapted from the Old French)

The Shepherd's Tale

Woman, you'll never credit what
   My two eyes saw this night . . .
But first of all we'll have a drop,
   It's freezing now, all right.

It was the queerest going-on
   That I did e'er behold:
A holy child out in the barn,
   A baby all in gold.

Now let's get started on the soup,
   And let me tell it you,
For though there's not a thing made up,
   It still seems hardly true.

There he was laid upon the straw,
   Will you dish up the stew?
The ass did bray, the hens did craw,
   I'll have some cabbage too.

First there was a king from Prussia,
   At least that's how he looked,
Then there was the king of Russia.
   This stew's been overcooked.

There they were kneeling on the ground.
   Come, have a bite to eat.
First I just stared and looked around.
   Have just a taste of meat!

Well, one of them he ups and says
   A long speech – kind of funny.
Here, what about that last new cheese,
   Is it still runny?

The little 'un, wise as wise could be,
   Just didn't care for that.
But he was pleased as punch with me
   When I took off me hat.

I took his little fists in mine,
   In front of all those nobs.
Fetch us a jug of our best wine
   My dear, we'll wet our gobs.

That very instant, as if I'd
   Had a good swig of drink,
I felt a great warm joy inside,
   But why, I cannot think.

Ah, this wine's the stuff, by Mary!
   When he's grown up a bit,
That little fellow, just you see,
   He shall have some of it!

We might have all been knelt there yet,
   Put a Yule log on the fire,
But suddenly he starts to fret –
   He'd begun to tire.

Then 'Sirs', his mother she did say,
   'It grieves me to remind
You that it's time to go away
   When you have been so kind.

'But see, how sleepy he's become,
    He's crying, let him rest.
You all know how to find our home
    Each one's a welcome guest.'

And so in silence we went out,
    But the funniest thing –
Those three fine kings, so rich and stout,
    Did wish me good-morning!

You see, love, that's how it began.
    The God born on the earth
This night's no ordinary one.
    Let's celebrate his birth!

                        James Kirkup
            (From the French of Raoul Ponchon)

Paul Revere's Ride

Listen, my children, and you shall hear
Of the midnight ride of Paul Revere,
On the eighteenth of April, in Seventy-five;
Hardly a man is now alive
Who remembers that famous day and year.

He said to his friend, 'If the British march
By land or sea from the town to-night,
Hang a lantern aloft in the belfry arch
Of the North Church tower as a signal light –
One, if by land, and two, if by sea;
And I on the opposite shore will be,
Ready to ride and spread the alarm
Through every Middlesex village and farm,
For the country folk to be up and to arm.'

Then he said, 'Good night!' and with muffled oar
Silently rowed to the Charlestown shore,
Just as the moon rose over the bay,
Where swinging wide at her moorings lay
The Somerset, British man-of-war;
A phantom ship, with each mast and spar
Across the moon like a prison bar,
And a huge black hulk, that was magnified
By its own reflection in the tide.

Meanwhile, his friend, through alley and street,
Wanders and watches with eager ears,
Till in the silence around him he hears
The muster of men at the barrack door,
The sound of arms, and the tramp of feet,
And the measured tread of the grenadiers,
Marching down to their boats on the shore.

Then he climbed the tower of the Old North Church,
By the wooden stairs, with stealthy tread,
To the belfry-chamber overhead,
And startled the pigeons from their perch
On the sombre rafters, that round him made
Masses of moving shapes of shade –
By the trembling ladder, steep and tall,
To the highest window in the wall,
Where he paused to listen and look down
A moment on the roofs of the town,
And the moonlight flowing over all.

Beneath, in the churchyard, lay the dead,
In their night-encampment on the hill,
Wrapped in silence so deep and still
That he could hear, like a sentinel's tread,
The watchful night-wind, as it went
Creeping along from tent to tent,

And seeming to whisper, 'All is well!'
A moment only he feels the spell
Of the place and the hour, and the secret dread
Of the lonely belfry and the dead;
For suddenly all his thoughts are bent
On a shadowy something far away,
Where the river widens to meet the bay –
A line of black that bends and floats
On the rising tide, like a bridge of boats.

Meanwhile, impatient to mount and ride,
Booted and spurred, with a heavy stride
On the opposite shore walked Paul Revere.
Now he patted his horse's side,
Now gazed at the landscape far and near,
Then, impetuous, stamped the earth,
And turned and tightened his saddle-girth;
But mostly he watched with eager search
The belfry-tower of the Old North Church,
As it rose above the graves on the hill,
Lonely and spectral and sombre and still.
And lo! as he looks, on the belfry's height
A glimmer, and then a gleam of light!
He springs to the saddle, the bridle he turns,
But lingers and gazes, till full on his sight
A second lamp in the belfry burns!

A hurry of hoofs in a village street,
A shape in the moonlight, a bulk in the dark,
And beneath, from the pebbles, in passing, a spark
Struck out by a steed flying fearless and fleet:
That was all! And yet, through the gloom and the light,
The fate of a nation was riding that night;
And the spark struck out by that steed, in his flight,
Kindled the land into flame with its heat.

He has left the village and mounted the steep,
And beneath him, tranquil and broad and deep,
Is the Mystic, meeting the ocean tides;
And under the alders that skirt its edge,
Now soft on the sand, now loud on the ledge,
Is heard the tramp of his steed as he rides.

It was twelve by the village clock
When he crossed the bridge into Medford town.
He heard the crowing of the cock,
And the barking of the farmer's dog,
And felt the damp of the river fog,
That rises after the sun goes down.

It was one by the village clock
When he galloped into Lexington.
He saw the gilded weathercock
Swim in the moonlight as he passed,
And the meeting-house windows, blank and bare,
Gaze at him with a spectral glare,
As if they already stood aghast
At the bloody work they would look upon.

It was two by the village clock
When he came to the bridge in Concord town.
He heard the bleating of the flock,
And the twitter of birds among the trees,
And felt the breath of the morning breeze
Blowing over the meadows brown.
And one was safe and asleep in his bed
Who at the bridge would be first to fall,
Who that day would be lying dead,
Pierced by a British musket-ball.

You know the rest. In the books you have read,
How the British Regulars fired and fled –
How the farmers gave them ball for ball,
From behind each fence and farm-yard wall,
Chasing the red-coats down the lane,
Then crossing the fields to emerge again
Under the trees at the turn of the road,
And only pausing to fire and load.

So through the night rode Paul Revere;
And so through the night went his cry of alarm
To every Middlesex village and farm –
A cry of defiance and not of fear,
A voice in the darkness, a knock at the door,
And a word that shall echo for evermore!
For, borne on the night-wind of the Past,
Through all our history, to the last,
In the hour of darkness and peril and need,
The people will waken and listen to hear
The hurrying hoof-beats of that steed,
And the midnight message of Paul Revere.

H. W. Longfellow

Miller's End

When we moved to Miller's End,
    Every afternoon at four
A thin shadow of a shade
    Quavered through the garden-door.

Dressed in black from top to toe
    And a veil about her head
To us all it seemed as though
    She came walking from the dead.

With a basket on her arm
    Through the hedge-gap she would pass,
Never a mark that we could spy
    On the flagstones or the grass.

When we told the garden-boy
    How we saw the phantom glide,
With a grin his face was bright
    As the pool he stood beside.

'That's no ghost-walk,' Billy said,
    'Nor a ghost you fear to stop –
Only old Miss Wickerby
    On a short cut to the shop.'

So next day we lay in wait,
   Passed a civil time of day,
Said how pleased we were she came
   Daily down our garden-way.

Suddenly her cheek it paled,
   Turned, as quick, from ice to flame.
'Tell me,' said Miss Wickerby.
   'Who spoke of me, and my name?'

'Bill the garden-boy.'
              She sighed,
   Said, 'Of course, you could not know
How he drowned – that very pool –
   A frozen winter – long ago.'

Charles Causley

The Demon of the Gibbet

There was no west, there was no east,
    No star abroad for eyes to see;
And Norman spurred his jaded beast
    Hard by the terrible gallows-tree.

'O Norman, haste across this waste –
    For something seems to follow me!'
'Cheer up, dear Maud, for, thanked be God,
    We nigh have passed the gallows-tree!'

He kissed her lip: then – spur and whip!
    And fast they fled across the lea.
But vain the heel, and rowel steel –
    For something leaped from the gallows-tree!

'Give me your cloak, your knightly cloak,
    That wrapped you oft beyond the sea!
The wind is bold, my bones are old,
    And I am cold on the gallows-tree.'

'O holy God! O dearest Maud,
    Quick, quick, some prayers – the best that be!
A bony hand my neck has spanned,
    And tears my knightly cloak from me!'

'Give me your wine – the red, red wine,
   That in the flask hangs by your knee!
Ten summers burst on me accurst,
   And I'm athirst on the gallows-tree!'

'O Maud, my life, my loving wife!
   Have you no prayer to set us free?
My belt unclasps – a demon grasps,
   And drags my wine-flask from my knee!'

'Give me your bride, your bonnie bride,
   That left her nest with you to flee!
O she hath flown to be my own,
   For I'm alone on the gallows-tree!'

'Cling closer, Maud, and trust in God!
   Cling close! – Ah, heaven, she slips from me!'
A prayer, a groan, and he alone,
   Rode on that night from the gallows-tree.

Fitz-James O'Brien

The Late Passenger

The sky was low, the sounding rain was falling dense and dark,
And Noah's sons were standing at the window of the Ark.

The beasts were in, but Japhet said, 'I see one creature more
Belated and unmated there come knocking at the door.'

'Well let him knock,' said Ham, 'Or let him drown or learn to swim.
We're overcrowded as it is; we've got no room for him.'

'And yet it knocks, how terribly it knocks,' said Shem, 'It's feet
Are hard as horn – but oh the air that comes from it is sweet.'

'Now hush,' said Ham, 'You'll waken Dad, and once he comes to see
What's at the door, it's sure to mean more work for you and me.'

Noah's voice came roaring from the darkness down below,
'Some animal is knocking. Take it in before we go.'

Ham shouted back, and savagely he nudged the other two,
'That's only Japhet knocking down a brad-nail in his shoe.'

Said Noah, 'Boys, I hear a noise that's like a horse's hoof.'
Said Ham, 'Why, that's the dreadful rain that drums upon the roof.'

Noah tumbled up on deck and out he put his head;
His face went grey, his knees were loosed, he tore his beard and said,

'Look, look! It would not wait. It turns away. It takes its flight.
Fine work you've made of it, my sons, between you all tonight!

'Even if I could outrun it now, it would not turn again
– Not now. Our great discourtesy has earned its high disdain.

'Oh noble and unmated beast, my sons were all unkind;
In such a night what stable and what manger will you find?

'Oh golden hoofs, oh cataracts of mane, oh nostrils wide
With indignation! Oh the neck wave-arched, the lovely pride!

'Oh long shall be the furrows ploughed across the hearts of men
Before it comes to stable and to manger once again,

'And dark and crooked all the ways in which our race shall walk,
And shrivelled all their manhood like a flower with broken stalk,

'And all the world, oh Ham, may curse the hour when you were born;
Because of you the Ark must sail without the Unicorn.'

C. S. Lewis

A wife was sitting . . .

A wife was sitting at her reel ae night;
   And aye she sat, and aye she reeled, and aye she
      wished for company.

In came a pair o' braid braid soles, and sat down
      at the fireside;
   And aye she sat, and aye she reeled, and aye she
      wished for company.

In came a pair o' sma' sma' legs, and sat down on the
      braid braid soles;
   And aye she sat, and aye she reeled, and aye she
      wished for company.

In came a pair o' muckle muckle knees, and sat down
      on the sma' sma' legs;
   And aye she sat, and aye she reeled, and aye she
      wished for company.

reel: a frame for winding yarn
ae: one
braid: broad
muckle: big

In came a pair o' sma' sma' thees, and sat down on
    the muckle muckle knees;
  And aye she sat, and aye she reeled, and aye she
    wished for company.

In came a pair o' muckle muckle hips, and sat down on
    the sma' sma' thees;
  And aye she sat, and aye she reeled, and aye she
    wished for company

In came a sma' sma' waist, and sat down on the
    muckle muckle hips;
  And aye she sat, and aye she reeled, and aye she
    wished for company.

In came a pair o' braid braid shouthers, and sat down
    on the sma' sma' waist;
  And aye she sat, and aye she reeled, and aye she
    wished for company.

thees: thighs
shouthers: shoulders

In came a pair o' sma' sma' arms, and sat down on
    the braid braid shouthers;
  And aye she sat, and aye she reeled, and aye she
    wished for company.

In came a pair o' muckle muckle hands, and sat down
    on the sma' sma' arms;
  And aye she sat, and aye she reeled, and aye she
    wished for company.

In came a sma' sma' neck, and sat down on
    the braid braid shouthers;
  And aye she sat, and aye she reeled, and aye she
    wished for company.

In came a great big head, and sat down on
    the sma' sma neck;
  And aye she sat, and aye she reeled, and aye she
    wished for company.

'What way hae ye sic braid braid feet?' quo' the wife.
'Muckle ganging, muckle ganging.'
'What way hae ye sic sma' sma' legs?'
'*Aih-h-h*! – late – and *wee-e-e* moul.'
'What way hae ye sic muckle muckle knees?'
'Muckle praying, muckle praying.'
'What way hae ye sic sma' sma' thees?'
'*Aih-h-h*! – late – and *wee-e-e* moul.'
'What way hae ye sic big big hips?'
'Muckle sitting, muckle sitting.'
'What way hae ye sic a sma' sma' waist?'
'*Aih-h-h*! – late – and *wee-e-e* moul.'
'What way hae ye sic braid braid shouthers?'
'Wi' carrying broom, wi' carrying broom.'
'What way hae ye sic sma' sma' arms?'
'*Aih-h-h*! – late – and *wee-e-e* moul.'
'What way hae ye sic muckle muckle hands?'
'Threshing wi' an iron flail, threshing wi' an iron flail.'
'What way hae ye sic a sma' sma' neck?'
'*Aih-h-h*! – late – and *wee-e-e* moul.'
'What way hae ye sic a muckle muckle head?'
'Muckle wit, muckle wit.'
'What do you come for?'
'For YOU!'

Anon.

sic: such
muckle ganging: much walking

Growltiger's Last Stand

Growltiger was a Bravo Cat, who travelled on a barge:
In fact he was the roughest cat that ever roamed at large.
From Gravesend up to Oxford he pursued his evil aims,
Rejoicing in his title of 'The Terror of the Thames'.

His manners and appearance did not calculate to please;
His coat was torn and seedy, he was baggy at the knees;
One ear was somewhat missing, no need to tell you why,
And he scowled upon a hostile world from one forbidding eye.

The cottagers of Rotherhithe knew something of his fame;
At Hammersmith and Putney people shuddered at his name.
They would fortify the hen-house, lock up the silly goose,
When the rumour ran along the shore: GROWLTIGER'S ON THE LOOSE!

Woe to the weak canary, that fluttered from its cage;
Woe to the pampered Pekinese, that faced Growltiger's rage;
Woe to the bristly Bandicoot, that lurks on foreign ships,
And woe to any Cat with whom Growltiger came to grips!

But most to Cats of foreign race his hatred had been vowed;
To Cats of foreign name and race no quarter was allowed.
The Persian and the Siamese regarded him with fear –
Because it was a Siamese had mauled his missing ear.

Now on a peaceful summer night, all nature seemed at play,
The tender moon was shining bright, the barge at Molesey lay.
All in the balmy moonlight it lay rocking on the tide –
And Growltiger was disposed to show his sentimental side.

His bucko mate, GRUMBUSKIN, long since had disappeared,
For to the Bell at Hampton he had gone to wet his beard;
And his bosun, TUMBLEBRUTUS, he too had stol'n away –
In the yard behind the Lion he was prowling for his prey.

In the forepeak of the vessel Growltiger sate alone,
Concentrating his attention on the lady GRIDDLEBONE.
And his raffish crew were sleeping in their barrels and their bunks –
As the Siamese came creeping in their sampans and their junks.

Growltiger had no eye or ear for aught but Griddlebone,
And the Lady seemed enraptured by his manly baritone,
Disposed to relaxation, and awaiting no surprise –
But the moonlight shone reflected from a thousand bright blue eyes.

And closer still and closer the sampans circled round,
And yet from all the enemy there was not heard a sound.
The lovers sang their last duet, in danger of their lives –
For the foe was armed with toasting forks and cruel carving knives.

Then GILBERT gave the signal to his fierce Mongolian horde;
With a frightful burst of fireworks the Chinks they swarmed aboard.
Abandoning their sampans and their pullaways and junks,
They battened down the hatches on the crew within their bunks.

Then Griddlebone she gave a screech, for she was badly skeered;
I am sorry to admit it, but she quickly disappeared.
She probably escaped with ease, I'm sure she was not drowned –
But a serried ring of flashing steel Growltiger did surround.

The ruthless foe pressed forward, in stubborn rank on rank;
Growltiger to his vast surprise was forced to walk the plank.
He who a hundred victims had driven to that drop,
At the end of all his crimes was forced to go ker-flip, ker-flop.

Oh there was joy in Wapping when the news flew through the land;
At Maidenhead and Henley there was dancing on the strand.
Rats were roasted whole at Brentford, and at Victoria Dock,
And a day of celebration was commanded in Bangkok.

T. S. Eliot

The Ballad of Billy Rose

Outside Bristol Rovers Football Ground –
The date has gone from me, but not the day,
Nor how the dissenting flags in stiff array
Struck bravely out against the sky's grey round –

Near the Car Park then, past Austin and Ford,
Lagonda, Bentley, and a colourful patch
Of country coaches come in for the match,
Was where I walked, having travelled the road

From Fishponds to watch Portsmouth in the Cup.
The Third Round, I believe. And I was filled
With the old excitement which had thrilled
Me so completely when, while growing up,

I went on Saturdays to match or fight.
Not only me; for thousands of us there
Strode forward eagerly, each man aware
Of tingling memory, anticipating delight.

We all marched forward, all, except one man.
I saw him because he was paradoxically still,
A stone against the flood, face upright against us all,
Head bare, hoarse voice aloft, blind as a stone.

I knew him at once, despite his pathetic clothes;
Something in his stance, or his sturdy frame
Perhaps. I could even remember his name
Before I saw it on his blind-man's tray. Billy Rose.

And twenty forgetful years fell away at the sight.
Bare-kneed, dismayed, memory fled to the hub
Of Saturday violence, with friends to the Labour Club,
Watching the boxing on a sawdust summer night.

The boys' enclosure close to the shabby ring
Was where we stood, clenched in a resin world,
Spoke in cool voices, lounged, were artificially bored
During minor bouts. We paid threepence to go in.

Billy Rose fought there. He was top of the bill.
So brisk a fighter, so gallant, so precise!
Trim as a tree he stood for the ceremonies,
Then turned to meet George Morgan of Tirphil.

He had no chance. Courage was not enough,
Nor tight defence. Donald Davies was sick
And we threatened his cowardice with an embarrassed kick.
Ripped across both his eyes was Rose, but we were tough

And clapped him as they wrapped his blindness up
In busy towels, applauded the wave
He gave his executioners, cheered the brave
Blind man as he cleared with a jaunty hop

The top rope. I had forgotten that day
As if it were dead for ever, yet now I saw
The flowers of punched blood on the ring floor,
As bright as his name. I do not know

How long I stood with ghosts of the wild fists
And the cries of shaken boys long dead around me,
For struck to act at last, in terror and pity
I threw some frantic money, three treacherous pence—

And I cry at the memory—into his tray, and ran,
Entering the waves of the stadium like a drowning man.
Poor Billy Rose. God, he could fight,
Before my three sharp coins knocked out his sight.

                                        Leslie Norris

Index of First Lines

Index of Authors

Acknowledgements

For permission to use copyright material the editor and publishers are indebted to the following:

George Allen & Unwin Ltd. for 'Stone Troll' by J. R. R. Tolkien from *Adventures of Tom Bombadil*; Angus & Robertson (U.K.) Ltd. for 'Legend' by Judith Wright from *Australian Poets: Judith Wright Selected Poems*; Collins Sons & Co. Ltd. for 'The Late Passenger' from *The Collected Poems of C. S. Lewis*; Faber and Faber Ltd. for 'My Aunt' by Ted Hughes from *Meet My Folks* and 'Growltiger's Last Stand' by T. S. Eliot from *Old Possum's Book of Practical Cats*; the author and Western Publishing Company, Inc. for 'The Alarmed Skipper' by James Thomas Fields from *Golden Treasury of Poetry*; the author and A. P. Watt & Son for 'Welsh Incident' from the *Collected Poems of Robert Graves 1965*; Harcourt Brace Jovanovich Inc. for 'Yarns' by Carl Sandburg from *The People, Yes*; David Higham Associates Ltd. for the following poems by Charles Causley: 'Miller's End' and 'Colonel Fazackerley' from *Figgie Hobbin* (Macmillan & Co. Ltd.), 'Nursery Rhyme of Innocence and Experience' from *Union Street* (Rupert Hart-Davis Ltd.) and for 'Take Heart, Sweet Mary' by Eleanor Farjeon from *Silver Sand and Snow* (Michael Joseph Ltd.) and 'The History of the Flood' by John Heath-Stubbs from *Selected Poems* (Oxford University Press); the author for 'The Shepherd's Tale' by James Kirkup from *The Descent into the Cave*; Macmillan, London and Basingstoke for 'Ghost Village by the Shore' by Raymond Wilson from *Rhyme and Rhythm* (Yellow Book) and Mr. M. Gibson and The Macmillan Company of Canada for 'Flannan Isle' by Wilfred Gibson from *Collected Poems*; the composers and Harmony Music Ltd. for 'The Ballad of Springhill' by Ewan McColl and Peggy Seeger from *Songs for the Sixties*; the author and Chatto and Windus Ltd. for 'The Ballad of Billy Rose' from *Finding Gold* by Leslie Norris; The Society of Authors as the literary representatives of the Estate of John Masefield and The Macmillan Publishing Co. Inc. for 'The Rider at the Gate' by John Masefield.

Every effort has been made to trace the owners of copyright and we apologise to any copyright holder whose rights we may unwittingly have infringed.